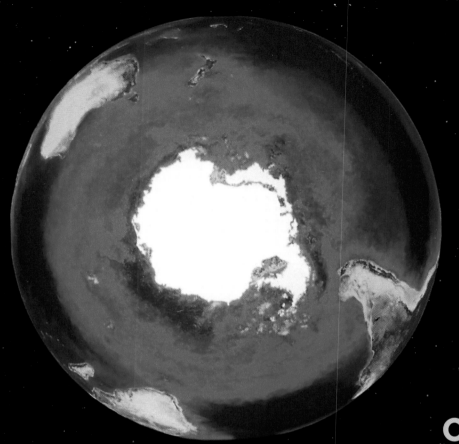

OUR AMAZING CONTINENTS

Continents are the largest pieces of land on Earth. There are seven continents. The largest is Asia. The other continents, from largest to smallest, are Africa, North America, South America, Antarctica, Europe, and Australia. Each continent's landscape has shaped the lives of its animals, plants, and people.

Library of Congress Cataloging-in-Publication Data
Sayre, April Pulley.
Hooray for Antarctica! / April Pulley Sayre.
        p. cm. — (Our amazing continents)
Summary: Introduces the continent of Antarctica, looking at its
geography, plant and animal life, weather, and settlement by humans.
  ISBN 0-7613-2152-7 (lib. bdg.)
  1. Antarctica—Juvenile literature. [1. Antarctica.] I. Title.
II. Series.
G863 .S254 2003
919.8'9—dc21
2002013684

Front cover photograph courtesy of © Wolfgang Kaehler 2002 www.kaehlerphoto.com;
Back cover photograph courtesy of © Fritz Polking/Visuals Unlimited, Inc.

Photographs courtesy of Visuals Unlimited, Inc.: pp. 1 (© NASA), 4 (© Fritz Polking), 9 (© Gerald
& Buff Corsi), 19 (top: © Gerald & Buff Corsi), 20 (© Brandon D. Cole), 22 (© Joe McDonald), 23
(top right: © Fritz Polking; bottom: © Joe McDonald), 26-27 (© Gerald & Buff Corsi); Photri, Inc.:
pp. 3, 6; Peter Arnold, Inc.: pp. 5 (© Michael Graber), 8 (© Gordon Wiltsie), 11 (top: © Gordon
Wiltsie; bottom: © Galen Rowell), 14-15 (© Gordon Wiltsie), 15 (© Gordon Wiltsie), 18 (© Galen
Rowell), 21 (bottom: © Doug Cheeseman), 26 (© Fred Bruemmer), 28 (© Kevin Schafer); Animals
Animals/Earth Scenes: pp. 10 (© David C. Fritts), 13 (© B. Bennett/OSF), 16 (© D. Allan/OSF),
16-17 (© NASA), 19 (bottom: © D. Allan/OSF), 21 (top: © Jung Aribert), 23 (top left: © Johnny
Johnson), 24 (top: © Johnny Johnson; bottom: © Bradley W. Stahl), 25 (B. Osborne/OSF), 29
(© Johnny Johnson), 31 (© Stefano Nicolini); ©Wolfgang Kaehler 2002 www.kaehlerphoto.com:
p. 12 (both); Corbis: p. 30 (© Morton Beebe). Map on p. 32 by Joe LeMonnier.

Published by The Millbrook Press, Inc.
2 Old New Milford Road
Brookfield, Connecticut 06804
www.millbrookpress.com

5 4 3 2 1

HOORAY FOR
ANTARCTICA!

APRIL PULLEY SAYRE

THE MILLBROOK PRESS, BROOKFIELD, CONNECTICUT

Emperor penguins

Hooray for penguins! Hooray for ice! Hooray for Antarctica, the wildest place on Earth!

Antarctica and its waters are home to seabirds, seals, and whales.

An iceberg bridge

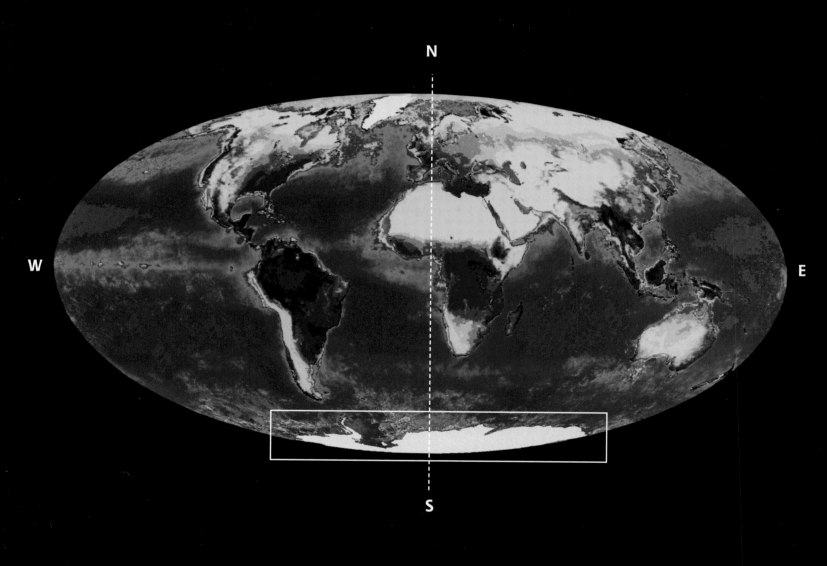

Antarctica is a continent located at Earth's South Pole.

Imagine a pole through the center of the Earth. The Earth spins, like a top, around this pole. The bottom of this imaginary pole is called the South Pole. That is where Antarctica is. Antarctica is surrounded by the Southern Ocean.

The continent closest to Antarctica is South America, about 600 miles (1,000 kilometers) away.

Antarctica is cold.

Crabeater seal

Antarctica is the coldest continent.

Its air temperature rarely rises above freezing. In winter, the temperature averages −80° F (-62° C). Sweat can freeze on a person's body. Icicles form on men's mustaches. In winter, human skin that's not covered can get frostbite in only a few seconds. People in Antarctica have to wear heavy coats most of the year. But seals stay warm because of their layer of fat, called blubber.

Its land is very high.

Transantarctic Mountain Range

Antarctica is Earth's highest continent.

Most of the land is high above the sea. Almost all the land is covered by a layer of ice about a mile and a half (2.4 kilometers) thick. This layer of ice makes Antarctica's surface even higher. Like all continents, Antarctica is made of land, with features such as mountains and valleys. Sometimes just the tip of a mountain will show above the ice line.

Antarctica has one of the world's deepest lakes, Lake Vostok. It is hidden under two and a half miles (4 kilometers) of ice. Strangely enough, Antarctica also has volcanoes. Mount Erebus, a volcano, erupted in 1998.

Glacial ice moving past South Ellsworth Mountains

The active crater of Mount Erebus

Icebergs can be different shapes and colors

Antarctica is icy.

Ice forms in the middle of the continent. The ice slowly slides from the continent's center to the sea. When it reaches the coast, the edges break off, forming icebergs.

Icebergs can be huge—bigger than large buildings.

In places, the ice doesn't break off. It stretches into the ocean. It is called an ice shelf. The Ross Ice Shelf and the Ronne Ice Shelf are the biggest ice shelves. They are each about the size of Texas.

It is windy and dry.

Antarctic ice skiing

Winds can blow for weeks in Antarctica. Antarctic winds can reach speeds of up to 200 miles (320 kilometers) per hour. Scientists often have to tie down equipment to make sure it does not blow away.

Most of Antarctica is dry enough to be called a desert— a polar desert.

It does not receive much snow. But the snow that does fall, stays. The weather is not usually warm enough for it to melt. This snow builds up over thousands of years. The weight of the snow on top turns the snow below into ice.

Work goes on in a snowstorm

Antarctica sometimes has strange, colorful skies.

In Antarctica you may see colorful shapes of light called fogbows, sun dogs, and mock moons. They are created when sunlight hits tiny ice crystals in the air. Splashes of color also light up Antarctica's dark winter skies. These winter colors are called the aurora australis, or the southern lights. These lights are similar to the aurora borealis, the northern lights, which are seen near the North Pole.

Sun dog

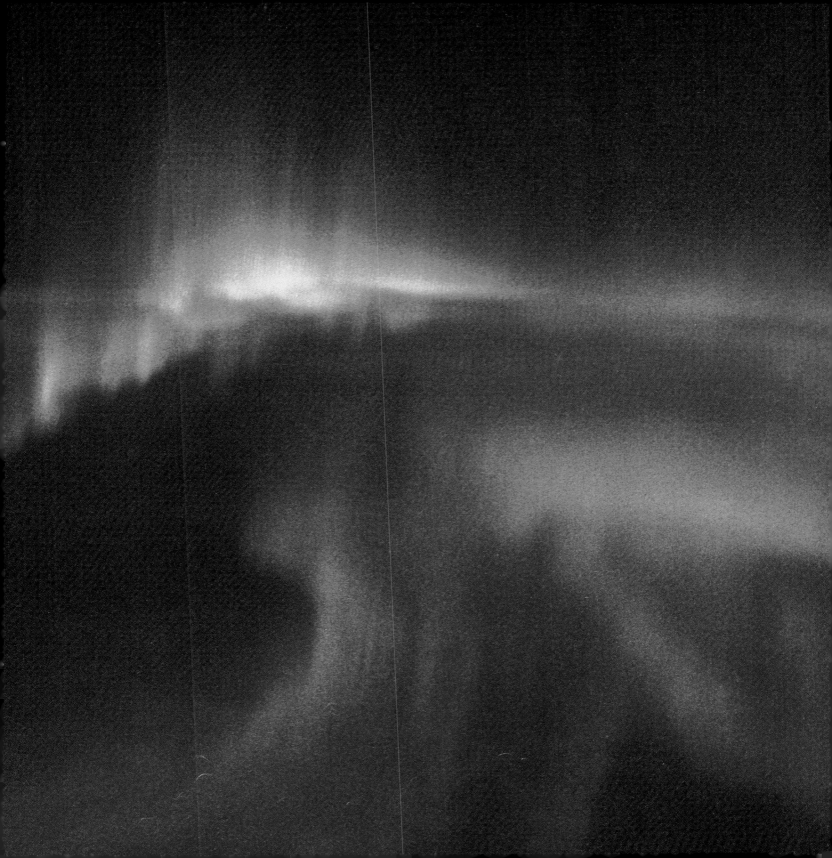

Algae growing in ice crystals

Antarctica has very few plants.

Cold, dry, windy, and dark for months, Antarctica does not have good growing conditions. But algae, a kind of tiny plant, grow in Antarctic snow. The algae look like red, green, or yellow stains.

Hairgrass and pearlwort

Lichens and mosses

More plants grow near the coast, where the weather is warm and the land is bare. Moss and lichens cover ice-free dirt and rocks. Antarctica has only two kinds of flowering plants: Antarctic hair grass and the Antarctic pearlwort.

A Southern Right whale, breaching

Antarctica has very few land animals. But many animals live in the surrounding ocean.

Antarctica's biggest land animal is a tiny insect called a midge.

The only other land animals are people and the animals people have brought. The Southern Ocean, however, is full of life. Tiny plants float in the sunlit water. Small ocean animals eat the floating plants. Bigger animals eat them in turn. Pink shrimplike animals called krill are food for fish, seabirds, seals, and some whales.

A midge

A krill

Rockhopper penguins

Penguins and seals live in Antarctica.

Penguins don't fly. They flap their paddlelike wings to swim. Seven kinds of penguins live on and around Antarctica: gentoo, emperor, king, adélie, Chinstrap, rockhopper, and Macaroni.

Penguins are seabirds. They raise their chicks on land, but they spend most of their time swimming in the sea. Penguins eat krill, squid, and fish.

King penguins

Gentoo penguin in nest with chicks

Chinstrap penguin with chicks

Antarctic fur seal with pup

A leopard seal gives a warning call.

Six kinds of seals live in Antarctica:

Antarctic fur seals, crabeater seals, Weddell seals, leopard seals, southern elephant seals, and Ross seals.

A Crabeater seal shares the waters of a hot spring on Deception Island with tourists.

Not many people live in Antarctica.

It is the least populated continent of all. Life is hard in Antarctica because it is so icy, windy, and cold. Most of the people who live there are scientists or people who help the scientists.

Tourists visit in January, which is summer in Antarctica. In summer, the night is very short. It is bright almost all day long.

Polar bears do not live in Antarctica. Antarctica is different from the Arctic.

Arctic polar bears

Antarctica and the Arctic are both icy, windy, cold places. But they are different in many important ways.

Antarctica is at the South Pole. The Arctic is at the North Pole.

Antarctica is a continent. The Arctic is not.

Antarctica is land. The Arctic is a region with mostly ocean. Much of that ocean is covered by ice.

Antarctica has penguins, but no polar bears. The Arctic has polar bears, but no penguins.

Weddell seal asleep on shore

Seals dive deep to search for food but come to shore to rest.

Seals eat fish and krill. Seals, in turn, are hunted by orca whales, who also eat some types of penguins.

Zodiac boats

Boats called Zodiacs take tourists from their ships to the shore.

Tourists and guides usually wear bright red jackets, so they can be easily seen if they lose their way. Not many people stay in Antarctica during winter. In winter, which is from May to July, the sky is dark almost all day long.

Scientists at the research stations plant their national flags with those of other countries on this international continent.

Antarctica is a special, wild place. Antarctica is not owned by any one country.

The continent of Antarctica is protected by the world. At first, several countries tried to claim it. But then many countries decided that Antarctica should belong to all Earth's people, so they worked out rules to share it. These rules, called the Antarctic Treaty, help protect the Antarctic environment—the waters, the land, and the animals.

ANTARTICA

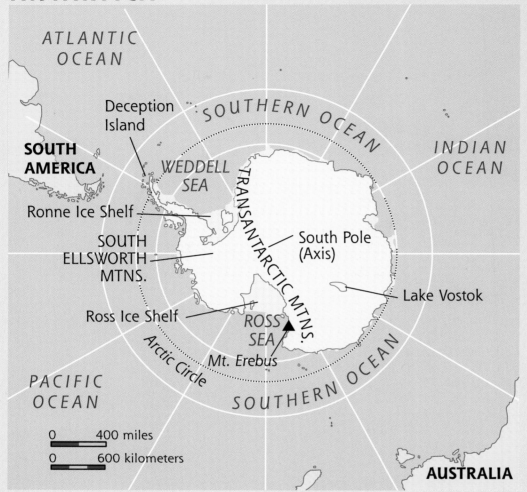

ATLANTIC
OCEAN

SOUTHERN OCEAN

INDIAN
OCEAN

Deception
Island

**SOUTH
AMERICA**

WEDDELL
SEA

Ronne Ice Shelf

TRANSANTARCTIC MTNS.

SOUTH
ELLSWORTH
MTNS.

South Pole
(Axis)

Lake Vostok

Ross Ice Shelf

ROSS
SEA

Arctic Circle

Mt. Erebus

SOUTHERN OCEAN

PACIFIC
OCEAN

0   400 miles

0   600 kilometers

AUSTRALIA

How do you get to know the face of a continent?

Books are one way. This book is about the natural features of a continent. Maps are another way. You can discover the heights of mountains and the depths of valleys by looking at a topographical map. A political map will show you the outlines of countries and locations of cities and towns.

Globes are a third way to learn about the land you live on. Because globes are Earth-shaped, they show more accurately how big the continents are, and where they are. Maps show an Earth that is squashed flat, so the positions and sizes of continents are slightly distorted. A globe can help you imagine what an astronaut sees when looking at our planet from space. Perhaps one day you'll fly into space and see it for yourself! Then you can gaze down at the brown faces of continents, and the blue of the oceans, and the white clouds floating around Earth.